D0722621

DYNAMIC
Denominators

Lisa Arias

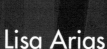

rourkeeducationalmedia.com

Scan for Related Titles
and Teacher Resources

Before Reading:

Building Academic Vocabulary and Background Knowledge

Before reading a book, it is important to tap into what your child or students already know about the topic. This will help them develop their vocabulary, increase their reading comprehension, and make connections across the curriculum.

1. *Look at the cover of the book. What will this book be about?*
2. *What do you already know about the topic?*
3. *Let's study the Table of Contents. What will you learn about in the book's chapters?*
4. *What would you like to learn about this topic? Do you think you might learn about it from this book? Why or why not?*
5. *Use a reading journal to write about your knowledge of this topic. Record what you already know about the topic and what you hope to learn about the topic.*
6. *Read the book.*
7. *In your reading journal, record what you learned about the topic and your response to the book.*
8. *After reading the book complete the activities below.*

Content Area Vocabulary

Read the list. What do these words mean?

common denominator

denominator

factor

greatest common factor

improper fraction

least common denominator

least common multiple

mixed number

numerator

scale

After Reading:

Comprehension and Extension Activity

After reading the book, work on the following questions with your child or students in order to check their level of reading comprehension and content mastery.

1. *When adding and subtracting fractions, do you add and subtract both the numerators and denominators? Explain. (Asking questions)*
2. *Can you add and subtract mixed numbers? Explain. (Summarize)*
3. *Why are common denominators needed when adding or subtracting fractions? (Asking questions)*
4. *Which strategy do you use to find common denominators? (Text to self connection)*
5. *Explain the different ways you can find the common denominator of two fractions. (Summarize)*

Extension Activity

Put your skills to the test! Write a story problem involving fractions with different denominators. You should try to have at least three fractions and two different denominators. After you write your story problem, give it to a friend or parent to try and solve. Don't forget to solve it first so you have the correct answer!

TABLE OF CONTENTS

FRACTION PARTS

Before we start, it is always best to review
a fraction concept or two.

Adding and subtracting fractions
with like denominators is quite tame.
Your aim is to add the numerators,
keeping the denominators the same.

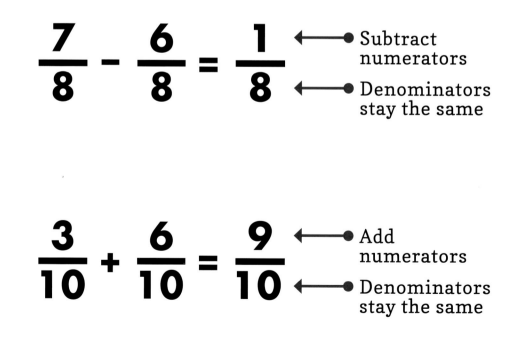

$$\frac{7}{8} - \frac{6}{8} = \frac{1}{8}$$

← ● Subtract numerators

← ● Denominators stay the same

$$\frac{3}{10} + \frac{6}{10} = \frac{9}{10}$$

← ● Add numerators

← ● Denominators stay the same

Add or subtract the fractions.

$$\frac{1}{4} + \frac{2}{4}$$

$$\frac{4}{7} + \frac{1}{7}$$

$$\frac{7}{9} - \frac{3}{9}$$

$$\frac{6}{12} + \frac{1}{12}$$

SIMPLIFY

Simplify before taking action
on a problem with a fraction.

This is very helpful to do, so that the fraction is in simplest form for me and you.

List the factors of each number, no matter how small
and pick the largest common **factor** of them all.

To simplify, divide the **numerator** and **denominator** by their **greatest common factor** and you are through.

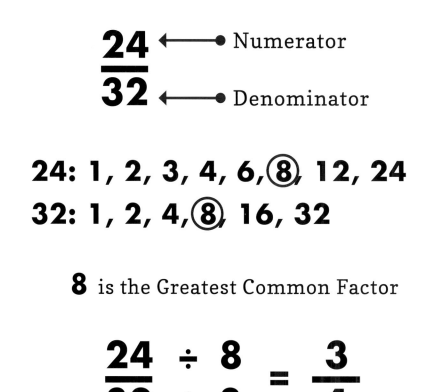

$$\frac{24}{32} \longleftarrow \bullet \text{ Numerator}$$
$$\longleftarrow \bullet \text{ Denominator}$$

24: 1, 2, 3, 4, 6, ⑧, 12, 24
32: 1, 2, 4, ⑧, 16, 32

8 is the Greatest Common Factor

$$\frac{24}{32} \begin{array}{c} \div\ 8 \\ \div\ 8 \end{array} = \frac{3}{4}$$

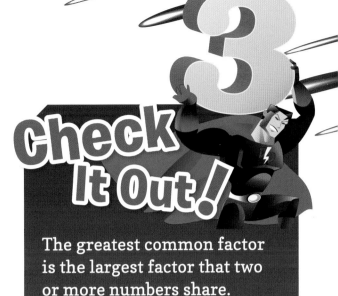

Check It Out!

The greatest common factor is the largest factor that two or more numbers share.

Find the fractions that are in simplest form.

$$\frac{2}{4}$$

$$\frac{1}{3}$$

$$\frac{30}{40}$$

Finding fraction equivalency is the catch when adding and subtracting fractions whose denominators don't match. Before we continue with that, let's take a peek at fraction equivalency.

Scaling is key to fraction equivalency. To do this, multiply the numerator and denominator by another whole.

The value of the fraction will not grow when this is done because you are just multiplying by a fraction of one.

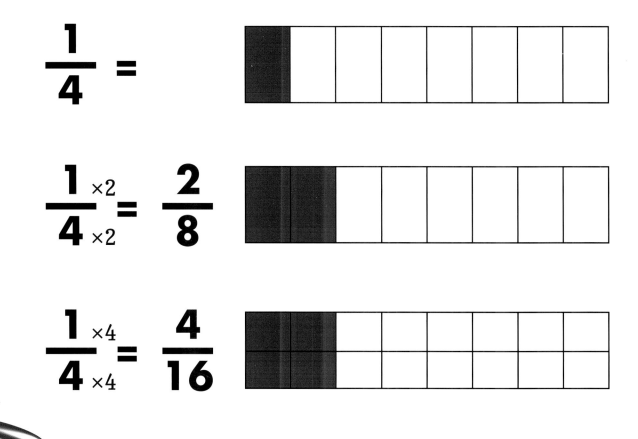

$$\frac{1}{4} =$$

$$\frac{1_{\times 2}}{4_{\times 2}} = \frac{2}{8}$$

$$\frac{1_{\times 4}}{4_{\times 4}} = \frac{4}{16}$$

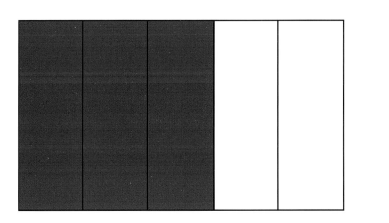

$$\frac{3}{5}$$

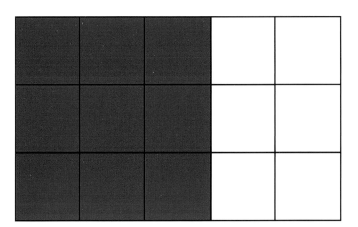

$$\frac{3_{\times 3}}{5_{\times 3}} = \frac{9}{15}$$

Why have a **common denominator**?

To add and subtract fractions with unlike denominators takes some care.

The denominators must be the same or things would be totally unclear.

Look at how things would be if the denominators do not agree.

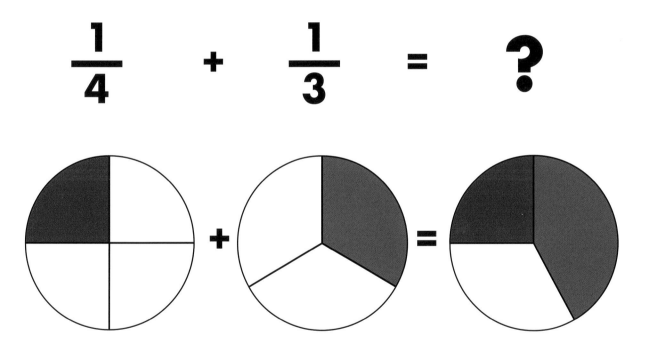

$$\frac{1}{4} + \frac{1}{3} = \ ?$$

LEAST COMMON DENOMINATOR

When the need for common denominators appear,
the **least common multiple** better be near.

Common denominators allow you to work in equal units making
things fair.

Find the least common denominator of $\dfrac{1}{8}$ and $\dfrac{5}{12}$.

8: 8, 16, (24), 32, 40, 48...
12: 12, (24), 36, 48...

24 is the least common denominator of $\dfrac{1}{8}$ and $\dfrac{5}{12}$.

What is the **least common denominator** for each fraction pair?

$$\frac{3}{8} \text{ and } \frac{5}{12}$$

$$\frac{1}{4} \text{ and } \frac{5}{6}$$

$$\frac{3}{5} \text{ and } \frac{7}{10}$$

$$\frac{4}{9} \text{ and } \frac{1}{6}$$

FACTOR TRICK

Time to learn a little trick to help make things go quick!

Take a look at these fraction pairs carefully. Take a moment to see that the smaller denominator is a factor of the larger denominator.

When this is the case, half the work is done and you will only need to **scale** one.

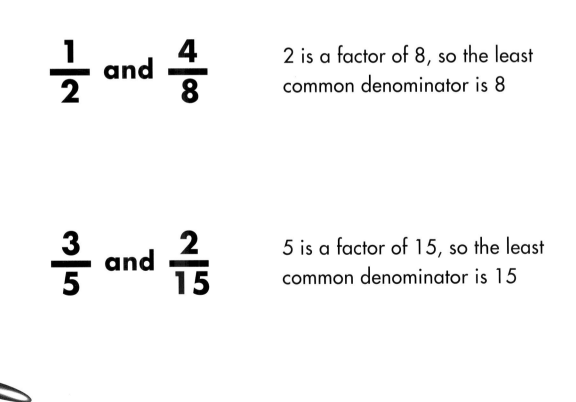

$$\frac{1}{2} \text{ and } \frac{4}{8}$$

2 is a factor of 8, so the least common denominator is 8

$$\frac{3}{5} \text{ and } \frac{2}{15}$$

5 is a factor of 15, so the least common denominator is 15

Which fraction pairs have the least common denominator hidden there?

$$\frac{1}{2} \text{ and } \frac{7}{10}$$

$$\frac{3}{4} \text{ and } \frac{5}{6}$$

$$\frac{2}{3} \text{ and } \frac{8}{9}$$

$$\frac{1}{12} \text{ and } \frac{5}{24}$$

Here is another trick to make things go quick.

If the denominators only share a factor of one, multiply the denominators together and you are done. Their product is the least common denominator of the pair.

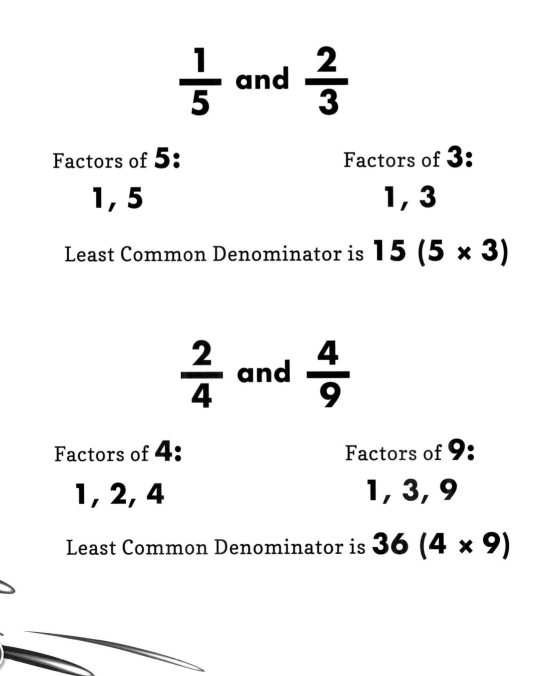

$$\frac{1}{5} \text{ and } \frac{2}{3}$$

Factors of **5:**   Factors of **3:**

1, 5   **1, 3**

Least Common Denominator is **15 (5 × 3)**

$$\frac{2}{4} \text{ and } \frac{4}{9}$$

Factors of **4:**   Factors of **9:**

1, 2, 4   **1, 3, 9**

Least Common Denominator is **36 (4 × 9)**

Use your new factor tricks to find the least common denominator for each fraction pair.

$\dfrac{4}{9}$ and $\dfrac{7}{8}$

$\dfrac{1}{2}$ and $\dfrac{5}{6}$

$\dfrac{4}{5}$ and $\dfrac{2}{9}$

$\dfrac{1}{4}$ and $\dfrac{2}{5}$

$\dfrac{7}{8}$ and $\dfrac{1}{4}$

$\dfrac{5}{9}$ and $\dfrac{1}{3}$

Once you find the least common denominator in question, it is time for some scaling action.

Multiply the numerator and denominator by the needed whole to create fraction pairs with matching denominators. Ready, set, go!

$$\frac{4}{9} \text{ and } \frac{7}{8}$$

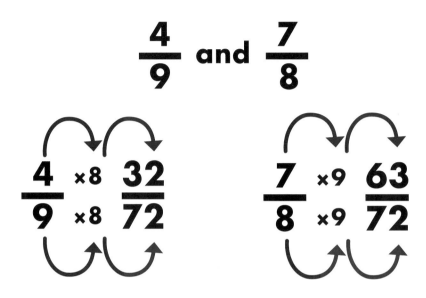

$$\frac{4}{9} \begin{matrix} \times 8 \\ \times 8 \end{matrix} \frac{32}{72} \qquad \frac{7}{8} \begin{matrix} \times 9 \\ \times 9 \end{matrix} \frac{63}{72}$$

Since 8 and 9 do not share any factors their LCD is 72

$$\frac{1}{2} \text{ and } \frac{5}{6}$$

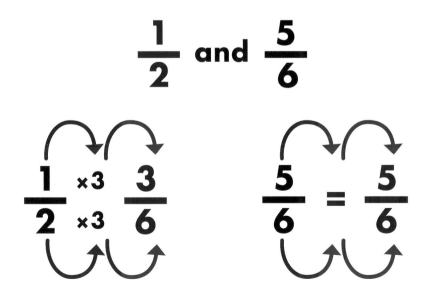

$$\frac{1}{2} \begin{matrix} \times 3 \\ \times 3 \end{matrix} \frac{3}{6} \qquad \frac{5}{6} = \frac{5}{6}$$

2 is a factor of 6, so 6 is the LCD (already done!)

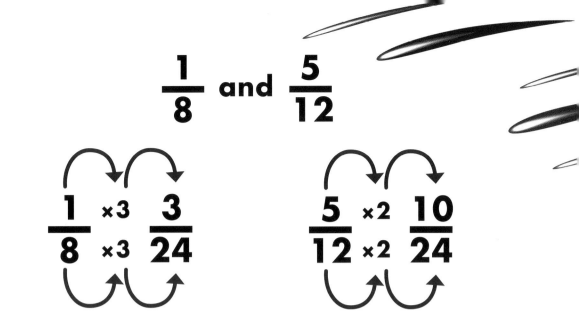

$$\frac{1}{8} \text{ and } \frac{5}{12}$$

$$\frac{1}{8} \times 3 \quad \frac{3}{24}$$

$$\frac{5}{12} \times 2 \quad \frac{10}{24}$$

8 and 12 share factors. Skip count to find their LCD.
8, 16, 24, 32
12, 24

Scale each fraction pair to like denominators.

$$\frac{5}{12} \text{ and } \frac{9}{24}$$

$$\frac{1}{10} \text{ and } \frac{3}{4}$$

$$\frac{2}{5} \text{ and } \frac{1}{4}$$

$$\frac{1}{2} \text{ and } \frac{1}{4}$$

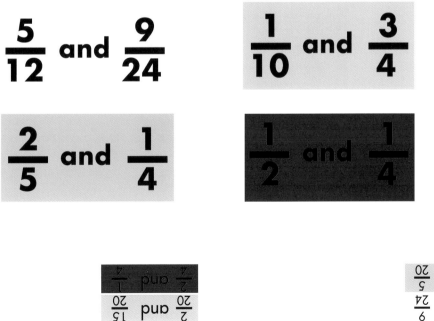

READY TO ADD AND SUBTRACT!

Time for some addition and subtraction fraction action!

Carefully follow each step one by one and simplify each answer when you are done!

1. Begin with both fractions in simplest form.
2. Scale each fraction to its least common denominator.
3. Add or subtract numerators.
4. Simplify your answer.

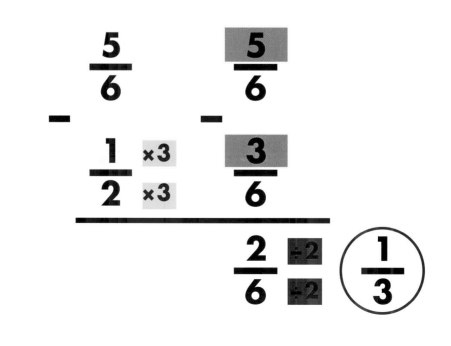

$$\frac{2}{9} \begin{matrix} \times 4 \\ \times 4 \end{matrix} \quad + \quad \frac{8}{36}$$

$$+$$

$$\frac{1}{12} \begin{matrix} \times 3 \\ \times 3 \end{matrix} \quad + \quad \frac{3}{36}$$

$$\boxed{\frac{11}{36}}$$

$$\frac{3}{5} \begin{matrix} \times 3 \\ \times 3 \end{matrix} \quad + \quad \frac{9}{15}$$

$$+$$

$$\frac{1}{3} \begin{matrix} \times 5 \\ \times 5 \end{matrix} \quad + \quad \frac{5}{15}$$

$$\boxed{\frac{14}{15}}$$

CONVERSIONS

Improper Fractions to Mixed Numbers

If you find an **improper fraction** after your addition or subtraction is complete, please rename it as a **mixed number** nice and neat.

Just take it one step at a time, and your answer will be just fine!

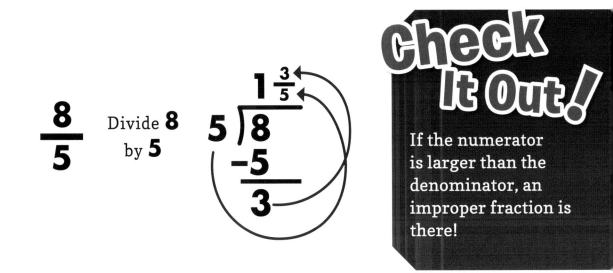

The remainder becomes the numerator and the denominator stays the same.

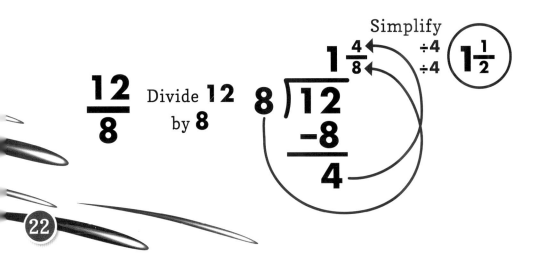

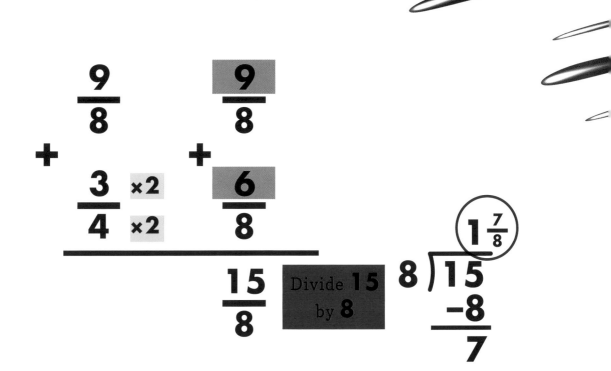

$$\frac{9}{8}$$

$$+ \frac{3}{4} \times 2 \atop \times 2$$

$$\frac{9}{8}$$

$$+ \frac{6}{8}$$

$$\frac{15}{8}$$

Divide **15** by **8**

$$8 \overline{)15} \atop -8 \atop 7$$

$$1\frac{7}{8}$$

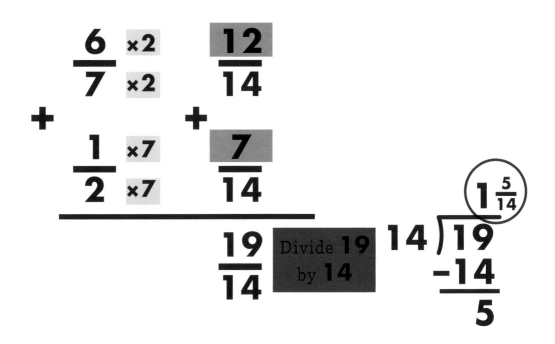

$$\frac{6}{7} \times 2 \atop \times 2$$

$$+ \frac{1}{2} \times 7 \atop \times 7$$

$$\frac{12}{14}$$

$$+ \frac{7}{14}$$

$$\frac{19}{14}$$

Divide **19** by **14**

$$14 \overline{)19} \atop -14 \atop 5$$

$$1\frac{5}{14}$$

Mixed Numbers to Improper Fractions

Let's get ready to take action
and change a mixed number to an improper fraction.

Doing this will make you glad
because all you do is multiply and add.

Multiply the whole number
by the denominator.

Multiply.

Add the numerator to
your answer.

This becomes your
numerator and the
denominator stays
the same.

Then add.

$$4 \frac{1}{3} = \frac{13}{3}$$

Change each mixed number to an improper fraction.

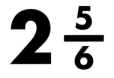

$$2\frac{5}{6}$$

$$4\frac{3}{8}$$

$$3\frac{5}{9}$$

$$6\frac{4}{7}$$

ADDING AND SUBTRACTING MIXED NUMBERS

Adding mixed numbers is easy to do.
All you do is break the problem into two.

First add the whole numbers together.
Then add the fractions.
Join the two parts, simplify if needed, and you're done!

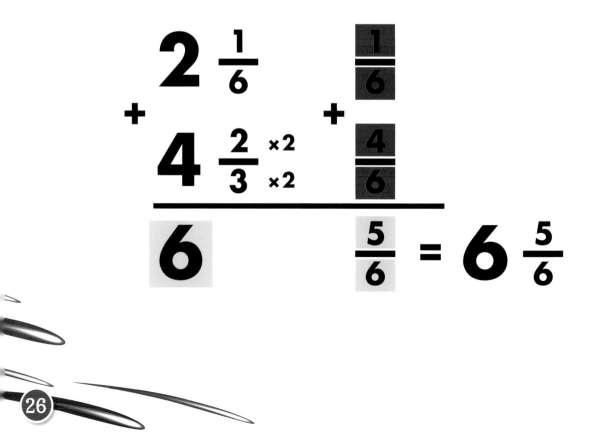

$$2 \frac{1}{6}$$
$$+ \quad \frac{1}{6}$$
$$4 \frac{2}{3} \begin{matrix} \times 2 \\ \times 2 \end{matrix} \quad + \quad \frac{4}{6}$$

$$6 \qquad \frac{5}{6} = 6 \frac{5}{6}$$

Add each mixed number.

$$4\frac{1}{3} + 3\frac{1}{5}$$

$$2\frac{1}{4} + 2\frac{1}{3}$$

$$5\frac{3}{7} + 4\frac{1}{2}$$

$$6\frac{3}{4} + 4\frac{1}{8}$$

When subtracting mixed numbers,
always begin with improper fractions.

This allows you to keep clear of a regrouping nightmare.

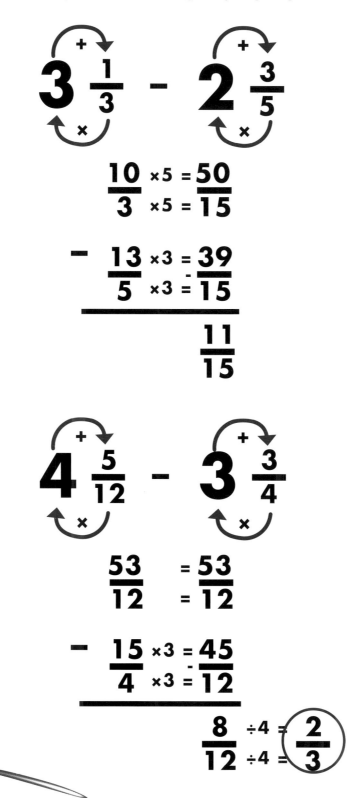

$$3 \frac{1}{3} - 2 \frac{3}{5}$$

$$\frac{10}{3} \begin{array}{l} \times 5 \\ \times 5 \end{array} = \frac{50}{15}$$

$$- \frac{13}{5} \begin{array}{l} \times 3 \\ \times 3 \end{array} = \frac{39}{15}$$

$$\frac{11}{15}$$

$$4 \frac{5}{12} - 3 \frac{3}{4}$$

$$\frac{53}{12} = \frac{53}{12}$$

$$- \frac{15}{4} \begin{array}{l} \times 3 \\ \times 3 \end{array} = \frac{45}{12}$$

$$\frac{8}{12} \begin{array}{l} \div 4 \\ \div 4 \end{array} = \frac{2}{3}$$

Subtract each mixed number.

$$4\frac{1}{6} - 3\frac{8}{9}$$

$$4\frac{1}{10} - 1\frac{3}{4}$$

$$3\frac{1}{9} - 2\frac{2}{3}$$

GLOSSARY

common denominator (kom-uhn di-NOM-uh-nay-tor): a common multiple that two or more denominators share

denominator (di-NOM-uh-nay-tor): the bottom number of a fraction that shows the number of equal parts of the whole

factor (FAK-tur): the number or numbers that are multiplied together

greatest common factor (GRAYT-esst kom-uhn FAK-tur): the largest number that is a common factor of two or more numbers

improper fraction (im-PROP-ur FRAK-shuhn): when a numerator of a fraction is larger than the denominator

least common denominator (LEEST KOM-uhn di-NOM-uh-nay-tor): the smallest common multiple that two or more denominators share

least common multiple (LEEST KOM-uhn MUHL-tuh-puhl): the smallest multiple that two or more numbers share

mixed number (MIKST NUHM-bur): a number containing a fraction and whole number

numerator (NOO-mu-ray-tur): the top number of a fraction that shows how many parts of the whole are taken

scale (SKALE): to multiply or divide a numerator and denominator of a fraction by the same value

INDEX

WEBSITES TO VISIT

www.sheppardsoftware.com/mathgames/fractions/
    LeastCommonDenomimator.htm
www.mathplayground.com/fractions_mixed.html
www.abcya.com/equivalent_fractions_bingo.htm

ABOUT THE AUTHOR

Lisa Arias is a math teacher who lives in Tampa, Florida with her husband and two children. Her out-of-the-box thinking and love for math guided her toward becoming an author. She enjoys playing board games and spending time with family and friends.

Meet The Author!
www.meetREMauthors.com

www.rourkeeducationalmedia.com

PHOTO CREDITS: Cover: © moorsky, niarchos

Edited by: Jill Sherman

Cover and Interior design by: Tara Raymo

Library of Congress PCN Data

Dynamic Denominators: Compare, Add, and Subtract / Lisa Arias
(Got Math!)
ISBN 978-1-62717-716-0 (hard cover)
ISBN 978-1-62717-838-9 (soft cover)
ISBN 978-1-62717-951-5 (e-Book)
Library of Congress Control Number: 2014935593

Printed in the United States of America, North Mankato, Minnesota

Also Available as: